For the Player, By the Player

Andrew Fiddner

For the Player, By the Player

An Examination of Online Video Game Communities

LAP LAMBERT Academic Publishing

Impressum/Imprint (nur für Deutschland/ only for Germany)

Bibliografische Information der Deutschen Nationalbibliothek: Die Deutsche Nationalbibliothek verzeichnet diese Publikation in der Deutschen Nationalbibliografie; detaillierte bibliografische Daten sind im Internet über http://dnb.d-nb.de abrufbar.

Alle in diesem Buch genannten Marken und Produktnamen unterliegen warenzeichen-, marken- oder patentrechtlichem Schutz bzw. sind Warenzeichen oder eingetragene Warenzeichen der jeweiligen Inhaber. Die Wiedergabe von Marken, Produktnamen, Gebrauchsnamen, Handelsnamen, Warenbezeichnungen u.s.w. in diesem Werk berechtigt auch ohne besondere Kennzeichnung nicht zu der Annahme, dass solche Namen im Sinne der Warenzeichen- und Markenschutzgesetzgebung als frei zu betrachten wären und daher von jedermann benutzt werden dürften.

Coverbild: www.ingimage.com

Verlag: LAP LAMBERT Academic Publishing GmbH & Co. KG
Dudweiler Landstr. 99, 66123 Saarbrücken, Deutschland
Telefon +49 681 3720-310, Telefax +49 681 3720-3109
Email: info@lap-publishing.com

Herstellung in Deutschland:
Schaltungsdienst Lange o.H.G., Berlin
Books on Demand GmbH, Norderstedt
Reha GmbH, Saarbrücken
Amazon Distribution GmbH, Leipzig
ISBN: 978-3-8433-5161-4

Imprint (only for USA, GB)

Bibliographic information published by the Deutsche Nationalbibliothek: The Deutsche Nationalbibliothek lists this publication in the Deutsche Nationalbibliografie; detailed bibliographic data are available in the Internet at http://dnb.d-nb.de.

Any brand names and product names mentioned in this book are subject to trademark, brand or patent protection and are trademarks or registered trademarks of their respective holders. The use of brand names, product names, common names, trade names, product descriptions etc. even without a particular marking in this works is in no way to be construed to mean that such names may be regarded as unrestricted in respect of trademark and brand protection legislation and could thus be used by anyone.

Cover image: www.ingimage.com

Publisher: LAP LAMBERT Academic Publishing GmbH & Co. KG
Dudweiler Landstr. 99, 66123 Saarbrücken, Germany
Phone +49 681 3720-310, Fax +49 681 3720-3109
Email: info@lap-publishing.com

Printed in the U.S.A.
Printed in the U.K. by (see last page)
ISBN: 978-3-8433-5161-4

Table of Contents

Chapter 1: Introduction   Page 3

Chapter 2: Who Writes this Stuff?   Page 14

Chapter 3: Super Smash Bros: Turning a Flaw into a Game.   Page 21

Chapter 4: Conclusion.   Page 39

Abstract

As a form of mass media, video games have been the object of distrust and even scorn. News reports and popular opinion would have many believe that video games lead to social isolation, that the objective of the player is to escape reality in the virtual world. Despite these opinions, the history of video games is one that involved communities. From the earliest days in arcades people played video games with the intention of playing with or against other people. In recent years the Internet has provided players with access to a much wider field of players and competition. As more and more games allow people to connect to distant players from the comforts of their own home, it would seem that the need to socialize has faded away. In reality, however, the Internet has spawned a great many communities entirely devoted to the play or discussion of video games. Often times these communities will center one specific game and exist entirely in the virtual sphere.

In the following paper I will analyze the communities surrounding the game of Super Smash Bros. Melee, a game originally designed for play in the home. Despite the fact that the game itself cannot connect to the Internet, players have created their own elaborate network of sites and forums. The analysis shows that even though players do not have to communicate with others to play the game, they still go out of their way to create relationships with each other. This paper also seeks to refine ethnographic techniques for the study of online communities. Rather than study the community on a single website or forum, I follow the members through many different electronic venues, tracing the method of thought regarding Super Smash Bros. Melee as the defining characteristic of this virtual community.

Chapter 1: Introduction

Video games are gaining an ever increasing foothold in the public sphere. The past ten years have transformed the video game from a private entertainment device to a much more public spectacle. Public venues and displays of video game prowess are becoming ever more common. 2001 saw the first ever "World Cyber Games" video game festival (http://www.worldcybergames.com/5th/history/WCG2001/wcg2001_overvi ew.asp). This international gathering featured contestants from all over the world chosen by regional tournaments in their respective countries. In addition to this tournament, the G4 television channel is devoted almost entirely to video games, and video game technology. It was launched in April of 2002, and became the fastest growing network in 2006, along with the number one podcasted network in America (http://www.g4tv.com/g4/about/index.html). Video games have certainly come a long way from their primitive and somewhat underground origins.

Possibly the biggest thing to happen to video games since their conception is the widespread adoption of online play. Whereas video games were originally the pursuit of people by themselves, or with another person, the Internet allows games to function with dozens, even hundreds of players at the same time. The Internet has also seen the rise of websites and message boards devoted entirely to the better understanding of video games. Most video game players are not seeking to isolate themselves from social interaction, but would rather discuss games with others who share their same level of enjoyment. In this way they are becoming active consumers, and not just passive zombies that are being manipulated by the medium. These groups of fans create large communities based around a particular topic, and seek to engage themselves more in it.

3

To fully understand the ways in which this new style of playing changes the dynamics of video games one must first understand the ways in which video games were played in the past, and the roots of the industry. Before I delve into that, I should first explain my personal relation to this topic. For me, the Internet is still a new thing. My parents never really had a decent computer while I was growing up, and we did not get any kind of Internet access until I was junior in high school. Therefore, I never developed an affinity for computer games, or Internet based games. My experience was always playing games that required a TV. My circle of friends all shared a love of playing these games with each other, and we would frequently gather at one another's houses and play the games with each other. Even if the game itself only supported two or four players, there could still be as many as eight of us in one room. The people not playing would either watch or find some way of entertaining themselves while the games were going on. For us, the actual game was not what made the encounter enjoyable, but the company we kept around the games. We enjoyed a very relaxed atmosphere, and even though we tried to win at the games, of course, losing never got in the way of our enjoyment.

Internet games, this is entirely my take on them based on my history with video games, are much more about the competition than the company one is playing with. This is because, in most instances, people do not personally know the other players in a game. The Internet is a powerful tool in that it allows people to connect with others from anywhere on the world, even if they have no prior knowledge of each other. This can greatly enhance a person's gaming experience, because it allows them to compete with other human opponents, rather than computer controlled ones, without going to all the trouble of gathering enough people to have a competition.

4

This first step even indicates an importance on the game rather than the company by the user. The person who decides to connect with strangers in order to enhance a playing experience is looking for just that, a better way to play the game, and is not concerned with the people they are playing with. There are, of course, games that attempt to create elaborate, on-line worlds, but these tend to have a different focus unique to them.

Short history on the Video Game Industry:

Dmitri Williams provides one of the most concise and complete histories of the video game industry I have come across in his book *Trouble in River City: The Social Life of Video Games*. He breaks up the history into five different stages starting as early as the 1950's. This era was started by the creation of the first computer programs designed primarily for entertainment. In general, these programs were created by computer designers as a form of mild entertainment for people while waiting to see their new inventions, or as a quick, easy way to show off the abilities of the newest computers (Williams, 2004: 27). He goes out of his way to point out that in the earliest years of video games, the people developing them did not think they could be used for profit, and thus the concept of a game on screen stayed out of the public eye for quite some time. As computers became more prominent, the hacker community started to adopt these games, and even develop their own (Williams, 2004: 28). These early computer programmers were mostly college students in technology based schools such as MIT. They were very interested in showcasing the powers of computers, and were big proponents of sharing their creations. Because of their philosophies, computer games still did not achieve any sort of public success, and remained a part of a very select community until the early 1970's.

5

In 1972, one of these early programmers, Nolan Bushnell, founded the company Atari, and released the first coin-operated, arcade game, *Pong* (Williams, 2004: 29). *Pong* became a wild success. The game had a very simple concept; players would control a white bar on one side of the screen, while a ball is bounced back and forth. The object was to keep the ball from falling off your side of the screen and forcing it to go off your opponent's, in other words, ping pong on a screen. Bushnell neglected to patent the arcade machine, so other versions of the game quickly began appearing in many locations around the country. It was not until 1977, when Atari released a home console, that they finally put a patent on the product. The Atari Company was not your typical corporation either. Most of the employees were either out of work computer programmers, members of local biker gangs, or pretty much anyone who was willing to work (Williams, 2004: 31). The work environment at Atari is important because it maintained the laid back sort of atmosphere that video games first materialized in. The early arcade machines they created were intended for use in bars and other locations where people gathered. Atari was without an efficient system for distributing its products or collecting funds. In fact, some of their machines were paid for by simply dropping coins a cut-in-half milk carton placed nearby (Williams, 2004: 30).

In 1978, Atari was bought out by the Warner Communications Corporation, and Warner applied its business sense to the fledgling company, drastically increasing Atari sales, and giving its products even more popularity (Williams, 2004: 34). By the early 1908's, arcades were reaching their peak of popularity in America (Williams, 2004: 34). Now, the games that Atari, and other companies, developed were not just limited to bars, but had gained enough notoriety that specific venues were being created to house these attractions. With the help of Warner, Atari had become a household name, and now people were lining up to play the newest games, or purchase the newest game system.

The rise of the arcade completely changed the way people viewed video games (Ofstein, 1991: 5). Arcades changed video games from a distracting pastime, to an intentional activity because now people would venture out in search of specific places to play video games. Most of the popularity arcades commanded was with younger adolescent males (Ofstein, 1991: 9). In their earliest days, arcades were not well received by the general public. In his ethnographic study of arcades, David Ofstein likens these early arcades to the pool halls of the 1940's and 50's; they were dimly lit, and often found in parts of town that most people considered to be unsafe (Ofstein, 1991: 9). Many parents considered them to be unsafe places for their children because they could not be sure what exactly was happening inside, and the playing medium was something completely foreign to them (Williams, 2004: 107).

Arcades not only provided people a place to find many different games, but it also gave people a new gathering spot. The very first arcades were very attractive to people who felt disenfranchised in their day to day life, and sought out places where they could be respected (Williams, 2004: 112). Williams claimed that these arcades created a meritocracy, a system where one's social status is determined by their abilities or skills rather than class, gender, race, etc. Therefore, it was not uncommon to see many different types of people within arcades, since the best way to be accepted into the groups that frequented them was to be good at the games (Williams, 2004: 108). The arcades were also toted as being remarkably acceptable to those willing to play the games, even if they were not particularly skilled.

7

As Ofstein explains, the games act as the bridging point for most social interactions within the arcade; the more you played with someone, the better chance you got to know them (1991: 10). This type of meeting and bonding over video games is very similar to the bonding that takes place within a modern game center. The key difference is that in arcades people are still meeting other people face to face, while the game occurs on the side. Game centers, with their focus on computer games rather than the older arcade machines, have people creating personas that exist only in the game world. You, therefore, have two levels of interaction taking place in this setting, once in the virtual world of the game, where players can communicate via keyboards or headsets, and the interactions that take place in the real world in conjunction with the games. Despite these differences, however, studies of arcades provide a good basis for the studies of game centers.

Despite the widespread success of arcades during the early 1980's, the popularity of video games eventually fell drastically. Williams attributes much of the decline to poor management on behalf of Atari, sacrificing their previous focus on innovation in an attempt to get more of their existing products into the marketplace (Williams, 2004: 40). The affect this ultimately had was that customers became tired of playing games that were either remade versions of ones that they had previously played, or just not as interesting, since they were attempting to release many more games than in previous years. Since Atari had no real competitors in the market, they decided it would benefit them more to try to saturate the market with existing Atari consoles, and maintain a monopoly, rather than create a new system (Williams, 2004: 40). This would ultimately alienate Atari's customer base, who were not as passive as the company thought it seems. Sales plummeted, and industry analysts were left with the impression that video games were simply a fad that was on its decline (Williams, 2004: 40). Even though the video game industry as a whole was falling apart, arcades managed to keep a fair amount of business throughout the mid 1980's, however, even they would not last. The independent atmosphere that made arcades so popular in the first place was lost once big name companies began purchasing the arcades and make them more "family oriented." Arcades moved into malls, and were given a much brighter atmosphere. Ultimately, the groups that had enjoyed the arcades previously lost interest, and the average age of arcade attendants lowered so that small children became the most frequent customers (Williams, 2004, 112).

The industry was revived in 1985with the advent of a new, home console, the Nintendo Entertainment System. Williams showed that by 1987, home video game sales had recovered to a profitable level, and that revenues in arcades were on a steady decline (2004, 44). In fact, there was a direct correlation between the successes of home video games versus the decline of arcades. As more and more people bought home consoles, less people decided to go out and play in arcades. Thus the 90's ushered in the era of home consoles. Several different systems were released by different companies, which forced developers to constantly improve upon their products, preventing the stagnant Atari scenario which almost ruined the whole industry. Any social patterns that developed through video games in the arcades faded away, since most of the games created during this time were intended for use in the home. This is not to say, however, that games had become a solitary experience. Many video games were made with the ability to support multiple players, even up to four by the mid-nineties. People could gather at one another's houses to enjoy these types of games, but it became very difficult to meet someone new by playing video games, since there was no longer a public venue. Some games even took on a "party" atmosphere. This is from my own personal experience, but there were several occasions when my friends and I would connect multiple TVs together and play large games with up to sixteen people. Of course we rarely managed to organize these events well enough to gather sixteen people in one place, but we did manage to this at least a few times.

The 90's also witnessed the stark rise in home computer technology, and video game developers were quick to take advantage of a new opportunity. The true power of personal computers was not evident until use of the Internet became commonplace, which allowed computers to do what no home console could do beforehand, provide players with access to large pools of competitors. Since then, online networks have become one of the most important factors for video game developers (Williams, 2004: 48). From an economic standpoint, online games have the potential to vastly improve profit, since companies can charge for the actual game itself, and then charge fees for use of online features. For instance, some games have monthly prescription fees that are required in order to play the game. Online games can also be used to appeal to a larger audience, mostly because these games are more easily catered to both sexes. In 1999, "online games were played by nearly even numbers of men and women, and 63% were between the ages of 25 and 44 (Williams, 2004: 49). A number of factors may be responsible for this, including the fact that video games on home consoles were targeting primarily at adolescent males, thus giving them little appeal to people outside that group. Computer games were more recent, and did not have a set audience before the Internet became popular, so there was not enough time to develop such a stigma. Also, since computers were already extremely widespread, getting people of any age/sex group was not a significant stretch.

The most important contribution online play and the Internet have brought to gaming is the development of online player-based communities. Games that may have only included online play options as an aside can sometimes develop large communities that make the game much more complex than the creators originally intended. One example is the game Half-Life. When it was first released it was praised for its engrossing single player game. The game did include a multiplayer option, but most players were not terribly impressed. Then, some enterprising individuals got access to the games programming, and modified the game to create a slightly different game. This is known as "modding," and is frequently a way people maintain game popularity by changing it. The mod they created was known as Counter-Strike, and became so popular that the company that made the original game hired the people who made the mod to work for them.

Online communities will even form around games that do not have online play. An example of this is http://www.mariokart64.com/mkdd/. The website is focused on a racing style game, and provides people with strategies, a list of the best times, and even videos of people achieving these times. It also includes extensive forums which let people discuss and debate different race strategies, or argue the legitimacy of the submitted videos, since authentication is very important when a person's reputation is at stake. These sites allow large social networks to be constructed through games that do not have this type of design built into them. The website, http://www.smashboards.com/, is a site devoted to bringing together people who enjoy the game Smash Bros Melee, a fighting game designed for play in homes. The site has several different forums within it, including regional forums, so players can discuss the game with those who live near them, and even a tournament location forum which let people post directions to nearby tournaments.

Game centers play a large role in this type of community; because it is there that these kinds of game tournaments are held. The tournaments are one of the biggest reasons these kinds of communities prosper in the first place. Large scale tournaments for games such as Smash Bros Melee give players something to aspire to, and provide them with a wealth of opponents. Normally it would be impossible for people who are communicating through Internet forums to determine who is a better player for a game such as Smash Bros Melee, since the outcomes of matches are affected by the participants. Having tournaments in which members of www.smashboards.com can compete with each other allows people to confirm whether a given tactic is effective or not. It also allows people to see who the best player is, and thus gain the most credibility on the site. Those who are infamous for winning are listened to the most because their advice is seen as having the most insight behind it, and thus would be the most useful. The tournaments also provide a meeting ground for people who may not have ever seen each other in real life. It is possible that the only interaction two members of the site could have before meeting each other is through communicating on the forums and watching videos of each other's matches. When they meet at the tournament they already have one notion of that person based entirely on their interactions through a machine. Game centers have become the newest way to enhance the experience of playing video games. They give players access to new technology and facilities. More importantly, they help virtual, online communities grow stronger by providing a place where these online acquaintances can become real ones.

In this paper I hope to demonstrate that video game players actively seek out the company of others, even if it is through a virtual medium. Many of the more recent games are created with the idea of online communities in mind, but even those games that did not have this intent still find themselves with a group of loyal followers. These groups are usually created and run by the players, and maintain a very egalitarian atmosphere. In addition to demonstrating the power of these communities, I also hope to show that an ethnographic style of examination of online communities is not only possible, but indeed useful in understanding the ways in which people are consumers of mass media.

Chapter 2: Who Writes this Stuff?

One of the biggest issues with writing about video games or even the Internet in general, especially from an anthropological perspective, is the lack of material written on the subject. Of course the reasons for this are manifold: the subject material is too recent, many people are not interested in the subject, and there is a stigma against video games and online technologies in our society that causes many people to be skeptical about these topics. The simplest answer is, of course, that this area particular area of study has only been available for about twenty years, and as such, academic materials have not appeared yet. However, there is a significant portion of the population that sees video games as a negative influence. They believe the games to be the cause of many problems, including leaving children open to sexual predators, and even degenerating people into gun-toting madmen. It would seem that most of the literature about video games that is easily accessible to the public is condemning them in one way or another.

The two most common types of complaints that arise over video games deal with either exposing children to unseemly content or unsavory characters. The content of video games, just like any form of entertainment, covers a wide range, and thus sparks many problems with those opposed to video games. One of the oldest problems people have had with video games is actually not the games themselves, but the types of people that play them. Even when games were in the early days of arcades, the crowds that these games attracted was hotly debated. David Ofstein's analysis of video arcades in the 1980's details the problems the general public had with the atmosphere that was created in these places. He explains that parents became very worried about video arcades because they had no idea what actually took place within the walls. The arcades themselves were dimly lit, to maximize attention on the screens, but the darkness caused more worry for parents, fearing that harmful people would be lurking in some hidden corner (Ofstein, 1991: 9). Williams also points out that many of the early arcades were places where people of all races or backgrounds could mingle (Williams, 2004: 108). All of these made the arcades a hot-bed concern for parents, who worried that their children may come into contact with any number of questionable individuals or substances.

This concern is not exclusive to arcades either. Ofstein compared the early kinds of arcades to pool halls of the 1950's and 60's, in that they were both establishments young people liked to go to that were somewhat dimly lit, and kept their actions out of the public eye (Ofstein, 1991: 11). The complaints geared towards pool halls were much the same as the problems people had about arcades. It was the classic case of people fearing the unknown. These are the same issues come up with most kinds of establishments when they are new. In the very early days of movie theaters, there was a large public outcry, because people feared that in the darkness many people would think they could perform elicit sexual acts and no one would notice (Williams, 2004: 120). Pinball parlors also received the same treatment. In fact, there was even a bill passed in the 1970's that outlawed pinball parlors in the city of New York (Williams, 2004: 134).

Williams termed this distrust of new technology as the "River City" effect (Williams, 2004: 10). This is a reference to the play *The Music Man*, in which a salesman attempts to start a music band with the town's children, and the parents work to thwart this new disturbance to their town. He cites many examples of unwelcome reactions to new forms of media through the past century and a half. These include movies, phones, television, and now the Internet. Movies began their life as entertainment for the lower classes. They were viewed as a crude form of entertainment, and deemed unsuitable for more refined people. This is why most of the earliest movies were shown in local storefronts, and drew small crowds. It was not until the film companies poured vast amounts of their own money into constructing elegant, grand theaters did the public's perception of movies begin to change. In large cities all across America, movie theaters became the premiere place to attend. Then the movie companies created the academy awards, which was such a grand, well-to-do affair, that people began to think of films as a legitimate art form. Having an official film academy gave movies an air of authority that had not before existed.

Television has never been very well received by the public. When television first became a prominent part of American culture in the 1950's it was touted as a family medium, even though debates were raging in Congress over juvenile delinquency and the media's contribution to that problem (http://www.museum.tv/archives/etv/F/htmlF/familyontel/familyontel.htm).

In those early days, television shows struggled to show programs that would be deemed "respectable" by most audiences. There is some kind of public perception, however, that the families that are depicted on television are somehow indicative or influential to real life families. This became clear when Dan Quayle declared that Murphy Brown, a then famous, unwed mother character, was an example of what was wrong with America (http://www.museum.tv/archives/etv/F/htmlF/familyontel/familyontel.htm).

Even today, television content is still hotly debated. There are limits to the types of content television shows are allowed to broadcast. Several studies have been done over the past fifty years to determine whether or not watching violent images causes people to become more aggressive themselves, but the results were questionable (http://www.museum.tv/archives/etv/V/htmlV/violenceand/violenceand.htm). Television is frequently cited as the reason for the breakup of the American family, which has been a constant outcry since some of the earliest days of television.

In more recent years, video games have received the blunt of public distrust. After arcades disappeared in the late 1980's, news was somewhat silent about video games, until the mid 90's. It was then that one of the first great controversies over game content erupted. The game in question was *Mortal Kombat*. *Mortal Kombat* is now a classic video game in the fighting game genre. The game offered no originality when it came to the actual gameplay mechanics, however. It was the same kind of fighting game people had seen before in earlier titles such as Street Fighter. What made *Mortal Kombat* infamous was the high level of gore the developers added to the game. The game introduced the concept of the finishing move, which allowed players to kill their opponents after they had beaten them. The finishing moves included such violent moves as pulling the opponent's head, including the spine, right off the body, and holding it up to the screen. This soon gained the attention of some anger parents, and the game started making the news. CNN ran an article about the game, claiming that the violence of video games had become "as much a part of a youngster's childhood as a trip to grandma's" (http://www.cnn.com/US/9803/26/media.violence/index.html? eref=sitesearch).

What made video games such a better target than television, movies, or music for these attacks was that people believed the games to be more influential to a young child's mind because the person using the media is taking an active role in the violence. There is also the fact that video games are the new medium on the market, and just as Williams has argued, there is going to be a negative reaction to such a medium.

After the events at Columbine High School violent media became the center of a great frenzy of complaints and debates. While the nation desperately tried to find a reason behind the killings of so many people the blame seemed to fall on the games and music the boys enjoyed. Doom, the shooting game that was blamed for some of the boys' issues, gained even more fame after the incident. As the complaints against violent games became more vocal, it even attracted the attention of the vice-president (http://archives.cnn.com/2000/ALLPOLITICS/stories/09/11/gore.entertainm ent/index.html). Other games began to receive the same treatment, including games that are not violent. A recent article from CNN claims that playing racing games turn people into aggressive drivers (http://www.cnn.com/2007/TECH/03/19/virtual.racing.reut/index.html). The article cites a study done, that claims that the men from the sample "who played even one racing game took more risks afterward in traffic situations on a computer simulator than those who played another type of game" (http://www.cnn.com/2007/TECH/03/19/virtual.racing.reut/index.html).

In addition to questionable content, video games have come under fire recently because of the people who play them, and the potential dangers they expose children to. These complaints revolve around issues regarding the Internet. People fear that children are becoming exposed to dangerous characters while communicating online; and that parents are unable to monitor or stop this from happening, because connectivity has become extremely easy. MSNBC's show, "To Catch a Predator" highlights the fears parents have of their children being easily susceptible to dangers that never used to be there before the advent of the Internet. The show's website also contains not only information on the show, and its purpose, but also an "online safety kit" that provides links to parents that are now worried about their children's safety thanks to the insights of the show (http://www.msnbc.msn.com/id/10912603/).

"To Catch a Predator" only touches on the fears parents may have about the Internet and their children. All of this falls onto the problem of people being able to conceal their identity others online. Video games, which are often perceived as a children's medium are often feared to be the favored stalking grounds of predators, sexual or otherwise. Therefore, whenever a news story about illicit material surfaces involving children and video games, a panicked response from the media is not far behind. The "Playstation Pornable" scare from last year had many people worried that the Playstation Portable, a small, portable gaming device, could generate a constant stream of pornographic images for unsuspecting children (http://kotaku.com/gaming/porn/playstation-pornable-plucking-hussies-out-of-thin-air-177476.php). In reality, there is nothing special about the Playstation Portable. The only reason it has the capacity to get porn is because it can wirelessly connect to the Internet; so it barely differs from any portable device with Internet capabilities, like a laptop.

More recently, another portable gaming device has garnered media attention with its online chatting function. The device in question is the Nintendo DS, which has the ability to connect to other, nearby Nintendo

DS's and send images back and forth. Users can also draw pictures on the screen using a special pen, and send those to other DS users nearby. Fox News ran a segment that claimed that this feature was attractive to child molesters. The story claimed that anyone within three-hundred feet could have access to children using the DS (http://kotaku.com/gaming/ds/can-the-ds-attract-child-molesters-234928.php). This article is ridiculous. The stated range of the DS by Nintendo is only sixty-five feet, so the claim that it can be three-hundred is either false, or better for Nintendo. Even if it can be used at three-hundred feet, the child molester in question would still have to be that close in order to communicate. Also, in order for people to send pictures back and forth to each other both parties need to have the image transferring program open, so the odds that a child will be using the chat function and happen to get within range of a child molester who is also using the same program are extremely low.

Video games have had to struggle to get respect from those who do not play them. The biggest fears about video games are that they will either expose children to unsuitable content or leave them open to dangerous individuals. Williams argues that many new communication technologies receive this kind of reception, as was evident from the history of movies and television. People who actively participate in video game based networks, however, are constantly aware that many in our society do not entirely approve of what they do.

Chapter 3

Super Smash Bros: Turning a Flaw into a Game

The Evolution of Gameplay

Sometimes the community that plays a game can drastically alter the way in which it is played. It is hard to find a better example of this than in the game *Super Smash Bros. Melee*. *Super Smash Bros. Melee* or Melee as it tends to be called, was released on December 3rd, 2001, and has continued to be a very popular game over the years, a feat which many games do not match. The game is for the Gamecube, a Nintendo system, and is actually the sequel to another game just called *Super Smash Bros.* While the game was mainly intended for use in the home, due to the fact that it was released on a home console that did not have internet capability, Melee has taken on an entirely new meaning thanks to the community of players that developed around it. They developed their own ways of playing it, and brought it to totally new level of play.

First, to understand the changes that people brought to the game, one must understand how the game itself is played. This was a particularly fitting game for me to analyze, because I have actually been playing it since it was first released, which has given me the insider's perspective, at least in some regards. I owned the original game and enjoyed playing it with my small group of friends, so I decided to buy the second when it came out. The concept of the games is very simple: characters from old, classic video games have to fight each other. There is no story or plot to the game; it was just made as an excuse to have already established characters, such as Mario and Luigi, fight each other. There are portions of the game that are designed for people to play alone and others that are intended for a group of people.

No matter which of the versions one plays though, the general concept of the matches remains the same, which is to knock opponents off the stage. The game is a fighting game, but unlike others of the genre, it does not rely on killing your opponent, like *Mortal Kombat* or *Street Fighter*. This allowed it to appeal to a wider audience, and not offend parents. Each stage is like a floating platform, and the objective is to knock characters off this platform, either so they cannot get back on, or all the way off the side of the screen (the camera stays static the entire time).

The game changed very little in the transition from the original to the sequel. Both games maintain the same concept of knocking opponents off the stage. Melee added several new characters and some single-player training games, such as a home-run contest where players have to see how far they are able to hit a large sandbag. The second game is obviously an improvement over the first graphically, and the controls are more responsive, but it was still a prettier version of the original *Smash Bros.* when it was first released. Player input, however, would soon bring a radical altering to the game major playing function.

As previously stated, my friends and I enjoyed this game a lot. Much of our free was spent playing the game with each other. It can support up to for people at once, which is a good number for a small group of people to enjoy with each other. My group of friends all shared a common interest in video games, and had been playing them our whole lives, so we can of course be very competitive people. This would lead to some heated matches, but that only made the game more enjoyable in our eyes. There was never a clear cut best amongst us, so we constantly vied for the top spot, which we could never officially determine. It never really mattered though, for us the enjoyment was the company, and the fact that we could bring out the most in the game, because we could give each other good competition. Melee is a game in which the possibilities for people to play by themselves can only last so long before it becomes stale. One could fight computer controlled opponents, but they are not particularly skilled or intelligent. Having ready human competitors that could provide a good match makes the game seem much more enjoyable.

Of course, we did not simply come together just to play a video game. The game was what we did while we were interacting with each other. The game, in this case, would act as a facilitator for the communication with my friends. Iain Simmons and James Newman concluded in their study that video games are typically used as a social pursuit, rather than an isolating one, and that the people who play them alone typically do so in the absence of better endeavors (Simmons and Newman, 2003: 3). This was not the only game that was played, of course, but it was the perfect game for crowds of more than two people, because it could easily handle four people at once, and it was a game that any of us could compete at. Even after I left my friends from high school and came here to Haverford, Melee was still an important part of our group of friends. Whenever I go back home, one of the first things I do is try to round up the whole group and play Melee. So, at least for me and my immediate group of friends Melee is more than just a game, but has become a sort of meeting point for us, much like a favorite bar or other such place. I did find people that enjoy the game here, but I do not get the same kind of enjoyment playing with people here, even though there are players here that are just as skilled as anyone I know back home, which is because the interactions with my friends from high school are based within the world *Super Smash Bros. Melee*. That is why, at one level, I was always an insider when it came to this game. However, I would soon find out that there is much more to this game than I initially realized.

Everything changed one day when I visited my friends who attended the University of Pittsburgh. One of my closest friends, Alec, met someone else who shared our same interest in Melee, named Garret, except that Garret was much better than any of us. It was through him that I was first introduced to a new side of Melee. When I first came home, I noticed that everyone was doing all kinds of crazy new moves that I had never seen before. When I asked about it, they told me that it was a new trick they had learned from Garret. Garret explained that it was called wavedashing. Wavedashing, as it turned out, is move people discovered based on a flaw in the game's programming. It is somewhat easy to explain, but very difficult to master. All characters have the ability to dodge things while they are in the air. This is accomplished with the simple press of a button, and the character will instantly move out of the way of a coming projectile. While dodging, characters are able to move slightly in any direction. Wavedashing takes this idea and does something else. To wavedash, one must jump, and then very quickly press the dodge button and move down. If done correctly, the character will not jump or dodge, but simply glide forward. The character does not make any movements, as if they are walking, but they still move side to side (it looks as if they are on a moving sidewalk). The true power to this move is that it tricks the game code. While the character does in fact move across the screen, the game thinks that the player is standing still. This allows the player to perform moves that are only possible while standing still on the move.

Wavedashing was the key concept that could drastically alter the way in which Melee is played. With its discovery, characters who are normally considered slow, such as Falco, can become much faster. I soon became acutely aware that this move gave people a distinct advantage over those who did not use it. At first, I was opposed to this concept. I thought that it was wrong to use a bug in the game to your advantage, as if it somehow took something away from the game. I was also upset that I had so much difficulty playing against those who used it. I know I said earlier that the game itself did not matter to greatly to me, that it was the company I was with, but I still got upset after losing many times. That's when I began asking them how to do this new move. After spending a lot of time playing the game with Garret over one winter break, I finally began to understand wavedashing. He also told me about other tricks that someone could that exploits the game mechanics. These included terms such as L-Canceling, in which a player presses the "L Button" on the controller just before the character lands from a jump. This allows players to quickly stop doing a move in midair so that they do not have any recovery time when they hit the ground, thus making them harder to counter by other players.

I asked Garret where he learned all of these moves, and he told me it was from watching videos of top ranked players online. Then he showed the website www.smashboards.com. The SmashBoards are a set of Internet forums that focus entirely on Smash Bros. The major focus is the second game, *Super Smash Bros Melee*, but there is a board devoted to the original. There is even a discussion section about the upcoming third Smash Bros game, *Super Smash Bros. Brawl*. At first, I dismissed most of this site, not really concerning myself with being a competitive player, which is what all the people posting on the site claimed to be. When I was thinking about different online communities to examine, this was one of the first that came to mind though, because it is such an expansive community, and yet it is focused mostly in one location. The main page of the SmashBoards claims to have "over 44,000 Smash Bros. fans from around the world come to discuss these great games in over 1.5 million posted discussions" (www.smashboards.com). This is the focal point of all discussion about Smash. In my searching for anything having to do with Smash Bros, the majority of the sites I found linked me to SmashBoards.

The more I investigated the site, the more I realized how in depth this community actually is. The most popular sections are those that involve discussion of the game's tactics. The "Melee Discussion" board and the "Character Specific" board give people opportunities to talk about new aspects of the game. "Melee Discussion" usually has about 19,000 active threads, while "Character Specific" will have about 13,000 (www.smashboards.com). Interestingly enough, the game itself can never change. PC games lend themselves very nicely to online forums such as these, because companies will occasionally update the game with a new batch of code, known as a patch. Console games, such as Melee, are final once they are released, so all the changes they are discussing are a result of people creating new strategies for a static game format.

The sheer number of terms people have created for this game is also impressive. One of the moderators, AlphaZealot, compiled a list of all the different terms, and provided an explanation for each of them in his thread "Wavedashing, L-canceling, All The Terms! Read First! Update 3/22/2007" located in the "Melee Discussion" boards (http://smashboards.com/showthread.php?t=42749). This thread is usually linked for people who are asking some of the more basic questions that the veteran crowd does not feel like answering over and over again. The thread is known as the Compendium of Knowledge, and even provides a brief history of the Compendium itself. It credits the original version to a poster named Bumble Bee Tuna, who wrote the first Compendium in 2003, which is only two years after the game was first released (http://smashboards.com/showthread.php?t=42749). This shows that people have at least been discussing these terms, which they created, for at least several years now. I cannot explain every single term, because the thread is actually several pages long, and would take up a considerable amount of space were I to put it in this paper. The vast majority of these terms, however, are created by the players. These concepts and tricks will not appear in the instruction manual or any Nintendo sanctioned strategy guide, because a good number of them were not intended to be in the game. These include wavedashing, crouch canceling, and L-canceling. They are some of the most important move people have adapted to the fighting within the game.

I have already explained wavedashing; and crouch canceling and L-canceling play on similar flaws within the programming. Crouch canceling, or CCing, is the act of holding down on the control stick so that when your character is hit. This prevents your character from being sent back very far, which is a great way to stay alive. Also, if the opponent is using a weaker attack, crouch canceling may keep you from moving at all. This allows the person doing the crouch cancel to quickly counter. The counter after a crouch cancel also has its own name, which is simply the crouch cancel counter, or CCC. L-canceling, meanwhile, is used when a character is just about to land after jumping. Usually, if a character is doing a move in mid-air, they will have to take a brief second or two to recover once they land. In that time they are unable to react. L-canceling requires the player to press the L button in any of the six frames before hitting ground. This will in effect stop the character from doing the recovery animation, because the L-cancel tricks the game into thinking that there was no air move (http://smashboards.com/showthread.php?t=42749). L-canceling, along with wavedashing, are some of the most important moves that a person can learn in order to play the game on a competitive level against the more seasoned players.

Distinguishing its Members

The divide between the average player and the "competitive" player is what creates the boundaries between the online Smash communities and normal game players. The majority of the community has a very elitist attitude towards the skills they developed for this game. There are numerous threads involving the justification of moves that exploit game mechanics. A typical argument against all these moves is that they were not intended for the game, and thus should not be used. Of course, such views are met with laughter and hostility on the SmashBoards. They have altered their style of gameplay to the point where it is necessary for them to use all of the higher levels of tactics to fully enjoy the game. Their experience with the game was altered due to their involvement with the community. In the "Today me and my smash buddy experienced... 'honor'" thread, Dylan_Tnga explains how he and a friend attempted to play the game without using any new moves.

"So with all the hype about cheap moves like wavedashing, L cancelling, edgehogging, fast falling, and short hopping and using high tier chacters being "dishonorable" that I have heard from scrubs around the world recently on these very forums, I decided to see what they were talking about."

(http://smashboards.com/showthread.php?t=100018,   posted
March 25, 2007).

His conclusion was that playing with "honor" was far less enjoyable, and the responses tended to agree.   Banksyayogame50 stated that the people Dylan_Tnga was trying to play with were ignorant and that he had not "come across anyone with that noob of a view in very long" (http://smashboards.com/showthread.php?t=100018,   posted   March   25, 2007).

In almost all forums regarding video games the terms "noob" and "scrub" are used to describe people who bad at the games, or have no idea what they are talking about. Noob is a shortened form of newbie, which was originally used as the insult, until people shortened it. Many words are abbreviated in online chat in order to communicate faster. Many computer games come with chat capabilities during gameplay to allow teammates to plan potential strategies. Players do not want to spend too much time typing out long messages to teammates during a match; so many common terms are shortened to make the typing faster. This practice then extends itself into the forums that talk about the games, and could potentially spread the terms to other forums. Newbie was one such term, used in almost every game. Words that are abbreviated forms of newbie include: noob, nub, nublet (although not shortened, seen as more insulting because of –let suffix), or any word that has "nub" written into it such as "nubtard" and "nubmaster general."

This difference between the "skilled" and "unskilled" players is what helps to define the community. The Internet presents a problem for anyone interested in doing ethnographic research because there is no physical location a researcher could travel to in order to examine a particular group of people. How can someone study a locale in a completely virtual world? The best way to view these communities is to take Benedict Anderson's approach, and see them as imagined communities. In his book, Anderson seeks to explain the origins or nations and nationalistic feelings. He notes the way in which the imagined aspect of nations allows for people to feel a sense of community, even though they will never know everyone in the community. He asserts that "all communities larger than primordial villages of face-to-face contact (and perhaps even these) are imagined" (Anderson, 1983: 6). Indeed, the difficulty for someone in Maine to know and interact with someone in San Diego makes it difficult for these people to have any kind of shared experience, and yet they would feel that same experience of being "American." In the same way, online communities are also imagined because the members will rarely ever see each other face-to-face, although this is not necessarily the case, as will be examined later. The Smash community is actually a worldwide community, spreading the ability of its members to relate to their shared experiences across national boundaries and even continents.

One of the links from SmashBoards takes people to the Global Smasher Compendium. This is a player created program similar to Google Earth that locates the home of any registered Smash player (http://smashboards.com/showthread.php?t=58804). The program is downloadable, and requires people to register their screen name, location, and character that will be displayed to others. The idea behind the creation of this program was to allow Smashers, as they like to refer to themselves, to easily find themselves in different areas, thus organization of tournaments would become much easier (http://www.smashwiki.com/wiki/Global_Smasher_Compendium).

There is a key difference between the national communities that Anderson speaks of, and the online ones, and that is the level of participation in each. Anderson argues that print media is responsible, in large part, for the creation of the national identities. He explains that newspapers that could easily travel to distant locations, and popular literature in which the hero is reported to fight for the good of "his people" help to create a sense of shared experience for the members of the nations (Anderson, 1983: 37). Whatever people in the nations feel they have in common is literally being told to them by the popular media around them. Online communities, on the other hand, come together because they already have a shared interest. The communities that spring about a particular game, like Smash Bros in this case do so because enough people enjoy the game, and want to discuss it with others who enjoy it.

In fact, these game communities are actually more closely related to the imagined communities of religion that Anderson mentions predated the nation. Part of the limitation of nations is that they have to be limited. Nations create artificial borders that distinguish themselves from other nations, meaning that a nation is also inherently limited in size and scope (Anderson, 1983: 7). Religious dynasties, on the other hand, could be as expansive as they wanted, as long as people were willing to participate in the religion. The spread of Christianity, Islam, and the Middle Kingdom all share these features. No matter how diverse the people who all joined in the community were, they would all remain connected through the use a similar language (Anderson, 1983: 12). Aspects of the religion can change as they travel around the world, but their language remained the same. For Christianity it was Latin, and Islam had it Arabic scriptures. Before the printing press, and the establishment of a literary common man, there was rarely anything printed in vernacular. All of the bibles were printed in Latin, while the Qur'an was forbade from being translated out of Arabic (Anderson, 1983: 14). The video game communities do not have to share the same language, since they usually encompass people from the US, several European countries, Japan, or Korea. Members are bound by their common interest. No matter how different two members of the SmashBoards may be in reality, they know that the other member also shares their love of the game, and they can talk about that. This aspect of the video game culture actually makes the online communities more "real" than the imagined nation-state. There is also a very high level of participation in online communities that ensures its members communicate with each other. This does not include simply discussing the game on message boards, but many other aspects as well.

Video Games as a Participatory Medium

The vast majority of the sites devoted to video games, not just Smash, are created by players, and encourage its members to assist the site by contributing. There is a collection of articles written by players specifically about all of the Smash Bros. games called the Smashwiki. All of the articles are user submitted, and are subject to editing by the rest of the community. This site boasts over 1500 articles, and in the span of a few days I noticed that the count of articles increased by about ten (http://www.smashwiki.com/wiki/Main_Page). It's a rapidly expanding site that all of the collective knowledge of the Smash Bros player base. The site contains several useful videos for those interested in increasing their Smash Bros skill. It also has links to other sites within the Smash community, such as the SmashBoard and Major League Gaming, or www.mlgpro.com.

Of course, this kind of collected center of knowledge regarding video games is nothing new. The website, www.gamefaqs.com is a huge online resource for people looking to find guides, hints, and cheats for video games. The concept of gameFAQs was first launched on November 5, 1995, and the domain name was registered on September 11, 1996 (http://www.gamefaqs.com/features/help/entry.html?cat=42). The site contains literally thousands of guides for video games of just about every age. It has information on games as old as *Football* for the Atari 2600, and covers all the way up to the most recently released games. Complete walkthroughs can be added as soon as a few days after the release of a new game. All of the information on the site is user submitted, and the cheats and hints were discovered by the users while playing the games, so the knowledge found here is all first-hand knowledge. The site's owners encourage people who use the site regularly to add their own submissions so that the body of knowledge can keep growing.

Henry Jenkins argued in his book that fan culture is one that encourages not just a passive viewing of whichever work they enjoy. He calls fan cultures a participatory culture, and points to the ways in which they take an active role in their enjoyment, and most fan groups seek to add something to their community. He shows how fans will often come to dominate the medium they are participating in. For instance, "The fan issued Hugo Award (named after Gernsbeck) remains the most valued recognition a science fiction writer can receive" (Jenkins, 2006: 138). Video games lend themselves even more to this phenomenon of participatory culture because the games themselves require participation. Therefore, to even talk about the game, necessitates a certain level of participation already.

Another extremely important difference between video game communities and other fan-based communities is that one's status in a game community is determined by one's level of participation. The vast majority of the discussions on the SmashBoards revolve around tactics, and how to improve one's play. Certain posters are going to hold more sway than others because they are known to be more skilled, or have previously put up useful bits of information. The most common way to improve one's skill is to watch the replays of the top players, and attempt to mimic their movements. www.youtube.com contains large collections of videos of matches from various tournaments. The matches that get the most views are those of players known to be good. The best players can be found by looking at various power ratings on the Smashwiki pages. These ratings are based on a number of different criterions, including final places at tournaments and the input of the rest of the community. For instance, the final matches between Ken and BombSoldier at a prominent tournament, the Jack Garden Tournament, have about 16,000 views each. Meanwhile, two of the lesser known players Aniki and Koto, only got 900 views. Also, the comments left on the video page for Ken and BombSoldier's video are people trying to analyze the match, and figure out what each player did (http://www.youtube.com/watch?v=0-kPc0EL9sU&mode=related&search=).

This importance on skill is what gives hierarchy to the online communities. The members of the SmashBoards are indeed somewhat elitist when it comes to people who are not in the community or those who deny the importance of the new tactics for Smash. However, when it comes to people already within the community, it is a rather egalitarian system. The way in which people can move up in the community is to display that they know a great deal about the game. This is done by having exceptional videos, showcasing one's skills, or providing many informative posts. The members of the boards who have been around the longest also tend to be better received by the viewing public, since it is assumed that they have had that much more experience with the game. Therefore, while it may appear, at first, that the Smash community does have a rigid hierarchy, it is entirely possible for anyone willing to practice enough to climb the social ladder.

Offline to Online to Offline and back to Online

Tournaments are the most important determining factor of a person's skill to the Smash Bros. players. Tournaments tend to be organized by the players themselves, and SmashBoards includes a tournament locator section in the website. This part of the site allows users to announce their tournament, when it's being held, and the location. It also gives them an opportunity to drum up enthusiasm for the tournament. If someone can advertise well on the message boards, and get many people excited there, it is more likely that the tournament the hold will have a greater attendance and attract better quality players. The number of people attending a tournament matters far less than the level of skill of the participants. Therefore, the tournaments that matter the most to people on the site are those that are guaranteed to have a decent number of good players attending.

Performance at the tournaments can be very important. At the most basic level, there tend to be cash prizes associated with the top places, so there is that incentive. More importantly, there is always the possibility of someone showcasing a particularly high amount of skill during a match. Hopefully for that player, someone brought along a video camera and recorded the match, or they did it themselves. They could then post the match online somewhere and demonstrate their abilities to the rest of the community. The videos people seek out tend to the final matches of tournaments, because it is assumed those will involve the most skill.

Much like Geertz's examination of the Balinese cockfight, the matches held at these tournaments can hold certain significance to the players. In his famous essay Geertz argues that the cockfight, for the Balinese is important not because it has a special function for the society, but because the fights can be viewed as a text for the larger Balinese culture (Dundes, 1994: 94). He then explains that men are not just putting their money or their carefully raised cock on the line when competing in a fight, but also their pride, although "no one's status is actually altered by the outcome of a cockfight; it is only, and that momentarily, affirmed or insulted" (Dundes, 1994: 110). In this way, the conflicts from the town are brought into the cockfights, which make certain fights much more interesting or deep. This can also be applied to the Smash community. Since the websites and message boards are where the players seek to gain attention for their tournaments, it only makes sense that the people attending the tournaments know each other before. They do not necessarily have to have met in real life before hand, but there is a good chance that they have talked to each other online. Internet forums, just like any other community will have conflicts and rivalries. Just like the cockfighting, game matches will embody any current conflicts happening in the message boards.

A person's performance at these tournaments are recorded and posted online. Even if no one makes a video of the event, there will at least be a page displaying the results. Any of the boasting done before the tournament (believe me, there's plenty) would have to be backed up at the actual event. Once the results are up on the website, people can see who can actually back up their words, and who was simply bluffing. Those that perform well enough will gain some prestige amongst the other players, while people who do poorly will remain obscure. No one is mean or hurtful to those that lose. In fact, many are all too willing to extend some advice, which in turn makes them look better. There are, or course, people who get on others' nerves, and these people would be the ones to get mocked, but they are rare. In general, there tends to be a high level of respect amongst the people responding to the tournament results pages.

Now the game has come full circle. It started out as a console game, designed for small groups of people to enjoy in their homes. Fans of the game exploited a series of bugs to enhance their playing, and thus make the game play very differently. These fans then created their own communities online that separates itself from the rest of the millions of video game players around the world through their acceptance of this new play style. In order to bring the players together, fans have created numerous sites that act as a knowledge sponge of all of the tips and tricks people have discovered about these games. Everything is run by the players, including the tournaments. The community then goes back to the real world to compete in these tournaments, which receive their importance from the online community. Finally, the tournament results find their way back into the online world, where the exploits of the players can be seen by all and discussed. This then allows people to debate more on the strength of particular characters or strategies, and thus the cycle begins all over again. Everything about the community, except for the game itself is run by the players. Video game fans are clearly not a bunch of slackers waiting to be hypnotized by the images in potentially dangerous games; rather they are a conscious group that will play the games the way they want to play them, and actively seek out others who share their enjoyment.

Chapter 4: Conclusion

An examination of the culture surrounding a video game can reveal a lot about the ways in which people enjoy their favorite pieces of media. Fans of games, or anything else for that matter, are not simple passive observers, rather they take an active role in their enjoyment. The fans will then manifest the enjoyment into large scale, online communities. These forums tend to be created solely by the players themselves, and reflect the active role they take in the consumption of their media.

Obviously, these video game centered communities do not have a central location. They are more a mental state, or imagined community like Anderson's. While there tends to be a main forum that may act as a focal point for all the interactions, aspects of the community exist not only on the message boards, but in sites that provide strategy guides and walkthroughs, groups of people who interact through the game in real life, and even the game world itself. More sophisticated games often provide the player with a large, virtual world in the game itself, where people can talk and interact. The most common example of this kind of game is the massively multiplayer online game, or MMO. World of Warcraft is a good example of a very popular MMO. MMO communities have all of the same aspects the Smash community had, but also include a world within the game itself, which adds another level of interaction. Often times, however, since the games were designed by the company to foster this type of group interaction, there is a sense that the community is not entirely run by the player. In fact, the message boards for World of Warcraft have less to do with players sharing their strategies on the game, and are full to bursting with pleas to the game developers to change some aspect of the game. With the company interfering with the creation of a coherent online community, the players do not seem to feel the same urge to work with each other, but instead seek the attention of the game management, since that is a more effective way of changing the game.

An ethnographic approach to video game or even online communities is entirely possible. The ethnographer has to realize that there is more going on than at just one website, or just in the game. These groups are communities of the mind, and can even extend beyond national borders. Many of the same, classical ideas of ethnography can still be applied to these situations, but the ethnographer has to realize that there is no central gathering point, and that the often sought after face-to-face relationships may be replaced by avatars and virtual bodies. In the future, these online communities will probably become much more commonplace. Instead of people bonding over a perceived shared experience, or simply because of the proximity of their local community, people will seek out others from around the world that share their same interests and create vast electronic communities. It will be important, then, for anthropology to adapt to these changes and develop ways of studying this new and ever increasingly important form of human interaction.

Works Cited

Anderson, Benedict. *Imagined Communities: Reflection on the Origin and Spread of*

    Nationalism. London: Verso, 1983.

CNN Interactive. "Study: Racing Games may Spur Risky Driving." April 9, 2007

    http://www.cnn.com/2007/TECH/03/19/virtual.racing.reut/index.html

Fahey, Michael. "Can the DS Attract Child Molesters?" *Kotaku* April 9, 2007

    http://kotaku.com/gaming/ds/can-the-ds-attract-child-molesters-234928.php

Feldman, Charles and Vercammen, Paul. "Youth Violence Puts the Spotlight on Mass

    Media." *CNN Interactive*. 9 April, 2007.

    http://www.cnn.com/US/9803/26/media.violence/index.html?
eref=sitesearch

Gauger, Eliza. "Playstation Pornable Plucking Hussies 'Out of Thin Air'" *Kotaku*

    9 April, 2007. http://kotaku.com/gaming/porn/playstation-pornable-plucking-

    hussies-out-of-thin-air-177476.php

Geertz, Clifford. "Deep Play: Notes on the Balinese Cockfight." *The*

    Cockfight. Ed. Alan Dundes. Madison: The University of Wisconsin

    P, 1994.

Jenkins, Henry. *Fans, Bloggers, and Gamers: Exploring Participatory*

    Culture. New York University Press, 2006.

Jones, Mark, Michael Liem, and Alex Penev. Mario Kart Double Dash
    Player's Page. 05 Dec. 2006 <http://www.mariokart64.com/mkdd/>.

MSNBC. *Dateline/*"To Catch a Predator" April 9, 2007.
    http://www.msnbc.msn.com/id/10912603/

Ofstein, Dovid C. "Videorama: an Ethnographic Study of Video Arcades."
    Diss. Univ. of Akron, 1991.

OptimusLime. "SSBM Ken (Marth) vs BombSoldier (Falco) JGT Finals
    Six" *Youtube*

    12 April, 2007. **http://www.youtube.com/watch?v=0**-
    kPc0EL9sU&mode=related&search=

Roselli, Mike. "Gore Takes Aim at Entertainment Industry for Excessive
    Violence."
    CNN Interactive. 9 April, 2007.
    http://archives.cnn.com/2000/ALLPOLITICS/stories/09/11/gore.enter
    tainment/index.html

Simmons, Iain and Newman, James. "All Your Base are Belong to Us:
    Video Game
    Culture and Textual Production Online" *Digital Games Research
    Association.*
    12 April, 2007. http://www.digra.org/dl/db/05150.26124.pdf

SmashBoards. www.smashboards.com

Spigal, Lynn. "Family on Television." *The Museum of Broadcast
    Communications.*

9 April, 2007.

http://www.museum.tv/archives/etv/F/htmlF/familyontel/familyontel.
htm

Tulloch, Marian and John. "Violence and Television." *The Museum of Broadcast Communications.* 9 April, 2007.
http://www.museum.tv/archives/etv/V/htmlV/violenceand/violencean d.htm

Various. GameFAQs. 05 Dec. 2006 <http://www.gamefaqs.com/>.

Various. Smashwiki. 12 April, 2007.
http://www.smashwiki.com/wiki/Global_Smasher_Compendium

Williams, Dmitri C. "Trouble in River City: the Social Life of Video Games." Diss. Univ. of Michigan, 2004.